Clarity:

I've been fighting for years as to who I really am. Trying to blend into my surroundings and accept the thing I am not; but I am supposed to be.

Or at least what I think I'm supposed to be.

Hell....I don't know.

All these questions without answers or even a small clue.

Taken the world around me for granted...No

It's the opposite

Isn't it?

My sacrifices were not for selfishness.

Pride? Standing for what is right?

Hate?

No....for change?

I don't know.

My back has lashes on it.

My mind plagued by every decision I've made.

Regret? Maybe

Self-awareness? Confusion possibly

An understanding of the depth within?

A rise to salvation?

Or a soul under siege?

Revelation first

..... Revolution

Revaluation to overcome

Searching for the Resolution

Caught between who I am

Who I'm supposed to be ... I think?

Mind, Body, Heart, and Soul:

Sits in a hospital in the fight for her life

Has trust issues developed by the narcissistic character of love

Has children and is only held together by God and his grace

Has the faith to never let anyone or anything detour that

Has all the love to give, but simply can't be accepting of the idea behind it

Has a baby boy and will give up life, in order to save his

Wishes to be a better father and show his sons how to become men

Only looks for the best in people.

Sees the world for what it's really worth...fucked

Can't take another positive outlook

Can't bare the weight of anything negative

Presents a false idea of happiness

Couldn't be happier with the blessings and gift of life from God

Looks for equality, for all

Questions the very existence

Can't accept death

Deathly understands death

My mind has questions, my body has cravings, my heart
isn't just mine, my soul is easily wavered

I'm lost and found at the same time

Confused but couldn't understand more clearly

Roughed edges, but still the most perfect shape

Scared and never more brave then this very moment

Mind completely fucked and viewed as sane

All of this together completes the creation that is me

My mind, body, heart, and soul

Spiritual Anatomy:

Roots = Your foundation of faith, your beliefs and the never ending cycle to provide life and secure your place as yourself in a crazy world.

Stem = Your persistence to continue to climb and reach. While still being flexible enough to sway in the wind taking on life's storms. Never braking and always still reaching.

Leaf = Showing the consistent growth, the things in the past that you have overcome. With the water of life that you've gathered from its storms.

Pedal = Exhibits the beauty and the journey. With some wilted and some perfect. The world has come to appreciate your peculiar and yet normalcy.

Representative:

I'm trying to challenge us at our absolute complete essence.

The things that make us human you and I.

If extasy is what's in between your thighs.

Euphoria has to be in the place you call "your mind"

I'm not like anyone else, Exceptional if you please. Not spitting game or simply bending on one knee.

Just want a minute or two of your time. I want to stimulate and ignite your senses.

Meaning I want to intrigue, learn you, intellectually.

I want my words to not just be something that you feed off of.

Rather you feel as if you can't breathe if any of my words don't carry love.

When I say "take off your clothes" what I'm really asking is "can you bare you soul".

When our lips meet, time becomes frozen, what I'm really thinking is "how could my heart be stolen"

When I say" I want to make love to you tonight" what I really mean is let our souls become one and take flight.

You see I think everything has been a misrepresentation of who I really am.

Perhaps some con artist, or collector with beating hearts in hand.

Don't you get it, that's not me.

I'm the guy at the very beginning who said he was intrigued.

Not by the clothes you wear or even what's underneath.

But by what you have in your mind, your faith, your strength, your beliefs.

After our encounter today I hope you feel encouraged, and not repelled

Knowing that I'm here to find the representative, that you call yourself.

Sports:

We are able to throw, clap, cheer and run before being able to form a sentence.

We are fascinated by the colors, lights and sounds surrounding an event.

It's a symbol of togetherness and what hard work and dedication can lead too.

For others it offers nothing but judgment ridicule and often categorizes players as "jocks"

For me.

Its more than either of those.

It's what bridged a gap between I and another male whose approval I longed for.

Sports allowed my father and I to be able to communicate in our own language.

My dad passing on his knowledge of the past and present of football and basketball.

Showing me Bill Russell, Julius Irving, Magic Johnson, Larry Bird, Archie Manning Jim Brown, Terry Bradshaw and so many more.

Putting what he learned from not only watching sports, but playing as well, into real life situations and understandings.

In this he showed his love of who he was where he was from and how proud he was have that background.

To have that culture.

My dad was born in 1953 in Mississippi.

He went through segregation, the integration of schools. Which in turn all came together setting aside thier differences through the love and spot light of sports.

Looking towards these so called "jocks" not for what they do on the fields and courts, but for what they do when they aren't on them.

My dad gave me three simple things that were applied to sports that he also applied to in life.

Do the best you can

As accurate as you can

As fast as you can

If I was smarter I wouldn't have waited till now to actually apply these to my life.

I have never forgotten these words or their order.

Not everyone can bounce a ball, not all people possess the hand eye coordination to hit something moving 100mph.

All you have to do is look closer and you'll see. This isn't just a sporting event.

It's a time in life bringing love into the world through perfect strangers. Its creating environments filled with memories that are heart dropping, breath taking and truly stunning all at the same time.

Its families built upon tradition honor and competitive love. Its friends drawn to causes behind the scenes.

It's a city, state or country sharing a piece of their lives, culture, and hearts through handshakes and tears.

I'd like to welcome you to the world of Sports.

Hands:

I forgot what yours use to feel like the peace the comfort the security

I longed for them to touch me I quivered when your fingers pressed against my lips

The tools used to build our home. Love being the materials used

Now I see the irony

"Stop that hurts"

"Let go of me"

Signs of the tools being used against me

"Shut the fuck up.... if you wake the kids up with your crying..."

Once, there was warmth from and within them

Now just cold and callused from the surfaces they keep making contact with.

The kids don't even matter to you anymore.

You show us your new found love.

I begin to fall

I wrap our son up with my body and brace for the impact of the floor.

Breathing was effortless around you.

Now I'm always fighting for air.

Suffocating slowly because I got your order wrong

Winded because you don't like to hear the baby crying

No longer vibrant No longer honored to be yours

Confused and unable to recognize who is looking back at me

Living in fear Always cautious as to not trigger you in any way

My worse decision

Your tools, your materials Used against our children

I loved you I love myself I love my children more.

So tonight, as you read this Know that I also have tools of my own.

And with these tools...

 you will never be able to destroy anyone else.

I See You:

As in through you. Or maybe not to that measure.

Maybe it's more of a simple visual stimulation that my brain perceives as a vibrant color.

The pallet of my taste buds dance in a query of complete misrepresentation of what taste really is.

My nerves are on end with the glance that you give me, rather I have taken.

The disposition of your mind intrigues me, the very thought of you not being in my sights makes me not want to be in the sight of the world.

You're pure, at least to me but it's hard to see through the veil of innocence that you hide behind.

All the cover ups don't speak as loud as your eyes do. They cry out in a bone chilling exhaust of sound.

I can see you completely.... I hope that you can see me too.

But my words aren't forming, either that or coming out wrong as if I'm trying to convert you.

Maybe crucify you as if I'm better
When just yesterday I spewed venom in a hand written letter.

I tried to be great and show you the love in my heart. Due to the irregular beat and no guidance, it's completely dark.

Wait I know what I have to say.... fuck!
I thought I did.

You remember the last time we talked? Literally just talked
About our lives, even imagined us taking that walk.

Down the aisle to say I do
Instead my lips firm up, my voice strengthens, and I yell "we're through".

Being so messed up, my mind is doing all of the thinking.
Not allowing my heart to be involved with making any decisions.

I want to speak to you, talk to you, or just be consoled.
I'm so in love with the thought of you I've just lost all control.

Working on my biggest issue you said "I don't communicate".
It's funny I started talking, which ultimately lead us to heartbreak.

"Evil thoughts keep running through my mind. Wonder how to make you feel the pain that's mine."

"Caught up in life like I'm looking at a flashing camera. Never thinking twice, and let my actions get the better of...me."

"Our should I say us and this life we have made. Given the fruits of life, and we still manage to make lemonade."

"Bitter and sour never anything sweet. Still holding our heads up never accepting defeat."

"Put our hands together and we begin to pray, with no honor for our father, so pretend again to play."

"This shameful game, I can't explain all the lives lost along the way."

"Joining the navy or the army trying to be all I can be. Coming home every night with hungry mouths to feed. Check the cupboards check the fridge...we ain't got nothing to eat. I'm so hungry I mean famished my kids look to me for hope. I work hard but still can't manage to keep myself afloat."

"Can you please, how bout you, please anybody spare some change. I'm on the streets with no home having war flash backs again."

"Are you listening to the news do you see the heartache. Another mother has lost a child, and six more were lost today."

"Wait...is it....do you see. The light at the end of this is the way it's supposed to be.

I feel a jerk then hear a noise I'm snatched back to reality."

"Think about all the people that I met through my journey. Then I stop and think wait.... All of them are me"

Father:

My father
What can I say....

The fact that we never got along...

So why is it I'm sitting here with so much shit on my heart?

When he was there I didn't want him around. When he wasn't around I wanted him there.

Torn and twisted in my feelings for someone I label less than a man. Meanwhile always secretly striving to be the very same man I see.

I've fought for so long to try to make him proud, feeling like my good wasn't good enough.

He was right it wasn't good enough. Every time I did something he said I could do it better.

Every time I said I could he said I couldn't.

Trying to survive in a world that I deemed insane.

My wheels spinning trying to make him stand up and say.

I'm proud of you.... or proud of what it is I lack.

Why the fuck are you constantly on my case.

Being examined under the microscope and picked apart in your petri dish of excellence.

The bar has been raised so high I can't even see, let alone reach it.

.......This whole time I couldn't see.

Now it's too late to say "Thank You"

You didn't accept my good because it's my best that you wanted. You set the bar so high so that I would be better than you in every aspect of life.

The words I feed off of and took to heart were only said so I could be inspired.

Others to light the fire under my ass do that you could say one day without a doubt.

"I am proud of my son"

Now here I stand in this pouring rain reading words people wrote about your life.

With tears in my eyes I can't even find the words in my heart to say "I'm sorry, I miss you...."

But most importantly thank you

For not only being a father.... but an even better dad.

It's On:

I come home my mind is racing. Simply because you and I have spent all day contemplating what we will do to each other.

I rush up stairs hoping to see you with high heels on and one of my favorite pairs... Of underwear

I have been thinking about you all day

and my heart is pumping my blood flowing feeling some type of way as in an animal.

I reach our bedroom and then there as I pre assumed.

You lay there with your heels and a robe on.

I look at you and swallow hard anxious to hear you speak.

Watching your lips move slowly as you form the words " it's time to eat"

Just then you slowly open your robe to expose yourself. I'm so excited, watching and thinking. "I can't wait for what's about to happen next"

There your body is completely exposed. Body glistening like the lights on a basketball court like I'm the bulls, looking at you baby.... yea my D rose

I'm sorry I meant to say rise, as I approach your body like a homeless man with a huge appetite.

I start kissing your lips biting the bottom one, nibbling and sucking on your nipples like I'm an addict waiting for my dealer to come.

You the fire cracker, my tongue the lighter licking your clit. Yea I'm making sparks.

I keep kissing I keep eating as you grip the sheets, believe me baby this is just the start

With my tongue in your mouth my dick in your hands.

It's clear to me now that you have other plans.

You flip me on my back and claw my chest.

I love it when sit on me, you always did ride the best.

Grab my cock and insert it deep in you. You bounce up and down fast and slow forcing me to moan too.

Your riding like it's your last ride and that pussy tightens up on me.

I can take it no more you keep hitting the tip I have to release.

I cum you cum our bodies shake in pure extasy.

I love coming home to you and getting the chance to fulfill my dreams.

Best Friend:

Words that are often said very loosely. Words that have lost their meaning for so many people. For so many people except for me. My best friend knows my every move. How I'm not complete unless they're in my life.

That I'm accepted for who I am, not what I've been through. That my past doesn't define me instead it helps me progress.In all of my short comings their faith in me is never waived. Soaked in blood from all the cuts and wounds of my life and yet I'm healed. Thank God for you my best friend, for the love and the faith. For the ever present truth of who we are and what we are together.

Through the tears the hurt the pain distance you still care the anger you're still in my corner. Good bad or indifferent you refuse to give up on me or us. This is something I could have never imagined. Your beautiful spirit matches the beautiful person you are. Your guidance and love for the world and God could never be matched.

I am in aww of you. It is you who makes me stronger, it is you who makes me think about how I should be better and it is you who always helps me remember who I am. It's you who continues to be everything I need.

You my very best friend.

Division:

Two separate entitie, One common goal

Zero chance of achievement

Every lie filling

Me with butterflies

Wounded sinking hearts

Clinging to each other for dear life

Simultaneously seeping the air out of each other's lungs

Twisted blades in each other's backs, mistakenly called love

Detonate inner reflections like wind-up toys

Perseverance is always inadequate to the glass house being built around us.

Strings on a guitar that only plays one note, still neither of us can hear

Everything that drove us, is now everything between us.

Everything between us, is what made us.

And everything that has made us has created....

Division

The Wager:

Mother Nature told God that she could match the beauty of one of his greatest creations. God asked if he could choose anyone of his creations "Yes" Mother Nature replied.

So God pointed and all day she has been trying her hardest and she still hasn't come close. What creation did God chose? It was you.

Just A Line:

I don't know if you've been told this but you are gorgeous. In the sense that you light up any room you step in. In the sense that you have been able to change the whole entire world for me and the way I see people and what true beauty is.

Random Quote of the Day

"I was taking a shit this morning, and thought of you."

Surrender

She said I love you
I replied "I love you

Looking back at her with all passion gone, replaced with lies

She said I miss you
I replied "I miss you too"

Words sent through text messages as I'm driving away.

She asked me how my day is
I told her fine

As if the time Im given to her has been assigned to me

I can't wait for you to get off
I replied me either,

knowing she is not the destination

She asked "where are you"
I replied "at work"

As she waits in the parking lot

Driving all night
Behind the wheel of her car and her mind

In search of what I once was

Dancing each night
With songs that never let her escape

Sleeping with the ghost
Of the only love she's ever known.

CHAVEZ LAPORTÉ CAMPBELL

Pain
Anger
Loneliness
Doubt
Prayer
Love
Forgiveness
Hope and
Surrender

Today is the day life changed for you. This day you will never forget. Every moment that you have lived has just been a guidance to prepare you for this particular day.

Every time you heard the words I love seem so small compared to now. Every touch you've every experience couldn't possibly prepare you for the touches you have yet to receive.

The words "complete security" have never been more of an understatement in your life.

You realize that God is real and very much alive. You question if you're ready and why he chose you with this great unbelievable task.

You question everything and everyone who has gone on before you.

You remember all of their teachings both directly and indirectly. And then you hesitate.

Will you be good enough, can you provide enough, will you be strong enough, will your faith be tested, will you be alone, and will you be loved in return?

Not realizing that this gift is a direct reflection of you. The beauty, the caring, the intelligence, the strength, the love, the sure resilience and the will to never stop pushing forward.

The complete faith and trust in God. The unconditional, untainted love that can only be given by who's images they were created after in the first place.

Today is the day you found out

You're having a babygirl.

Eccentric:

It's crazy

A simple hello has us here

At a place neither of us expected

This intertwined road, all our fears, yet pleasure and contentment

Nostalgia and erratic breathing as my hand meets your face.

We open our mouths and speak words at the same time.

We both laugh

"You go"

"No go ahead babe"

The environment around us is in our control

People disappear

Music plays in a genre created only by our hearts.

Our breathing synchronizes

We draw closer

Our eyes close

We lean our heads against each other

Pulse intensely vibrating throughout or bodies like sonar.

"Can I kiss you"

"You never have to ask"

Our lips begin to touch

We stop breathing

Lips clasp

My face goes numb

The fervid feeling awakes me....

I roll over

You're not here

I'm alone

I see you every week

I talk to you everyday

My love hidden with

It's time, I let you in.

I have something to say

"It's crazy......"

$$\mathcal{J}....$$

The love I have for you is never underestimated

I always try to let you know but it seems like it gets lost in translation.

I wish I was more of the man you need me to be. But you are the one who loves and always believes in me.

There are times where it seems our relationship is tested, but every morning I wake up I realized that I'm truly blessed.

To be given a new friend, love and a life. I know now that I'll never face this strife: alone.

With you by my side we will endure life,

Not fully having guide: lines

To follow we make up our own rules to follow: hearts

This way you and I remain forever and will never be torn apart: paper

Our love for each other wasn't born it was created.

Crazy:

I'm sick of feeling crazy about you and I.

Our world's no longer co exist we are two separate entities.

The world as we know it is so fucked up that the trust we once had is now just a memory.

I loved you more than anyone else ever should and now I will pay the ultimate price by losing myself.

I guess what goes around comes around.

I deserve every bit of this I deserve to feel the hurt that I have bestowed unto others.

I deserve to have my faith in relationships shattered because I am a heartless being.

So why is it that I always feel so unemotional, out of control that my soul is black and my heart is stone.

Or could it be that I do not love anyone not even myself.

So many days have past I can't get a grip on reality haunted by my nightmares of "happy ever after" so I choose not to sleep.

While you lay here dreaming of other people but you snuggle up with me.

Silence is all throughout our house, phones don't make a sound, heartbeats aren't present and in some cases I can't even here you breath.

Like your some type of alien.

That youre practicing so you can accomplish a goal.

Of being completely dead to me.

Real Or Fake:

I'm confused how to feel with the words you say to me.
Saying that you want a real man, but fake is all I see in front of me.
All over the world airing your dirty laundry in the streets.
Posing half naked on Facebook just to see how many pokes you can get in a week.

You insist that it's for women who are like you.
But what about all the women who are beautiful, and have brains too.
Expecting to get self-confidence from a world that is sex driven.
It's called self-esteem, so shouldn't it be self-driven?

Flirting with everyone and talking nasty on your post in clear view.
I knew a woman like that but I only see her when I look in my rear view.
All these women keep talking that a good man is hard to find.
Well maybe show us more than your body, let me see the power of your mind.

Men only want one thing from a woman and it's what you show us
Maybe a little less tits and ass and a little more "grown up"
Meaning you handle your business and send me pictures of you
You're fully clothed at worked with an empire behind you.

Ladies you are more than just a good piece of ass
Show these men that you have everything he wish he had.
Show them your independence and strength
Show him how you moved up the ladder but never flashed your tits.
Again you say you're looking for real man,
Thousands of people comment on your naked pics, but all of them are just fans.

This is not the players club, and you don't have to do something strange for some change.
Respect yourself and me that way at the end of the night I know who you are, and your name.

Want a real man then stop being fake.Its ok to be that business woman, music woman, or magazine
writer with your own page.
Be the beautiful woman God created you to be.
There's nothing fake about a real woman, that is what's attractive to me.

Perception:

Everyone has their vantage points.

Things that lead you to believe or assume numerous possibilities. Wait, maybe it's more than that, maybe its straight up ignorance. We look around and see things and we automatically draw up a conclusion to the story.

These things are what help us reinforce stereotypes, of race, age, gender, politics, and spiritual beliefs.

Like black people love chicken and watermelon.

Are you fucking serious,

if you truly hung out with black people you would know that we would have some orange or grape pop also.

Wait not my point.

How about white people don't have rythem.

Shit....not a good one eiter.

Fucking racist perception.

All politicians are evil just because we are poor and they run the country and get paid off of our hard earned money that doesn't......

wait.... ok bad example.

What about a guy helping a young lady

You think he's trying to hit on her.

Most cases you're probably right, wait I mean wrong.

Because he only wants her number....

DAMN YOU PERCEPTION

you have mislead me again.

Love is.....

Being in love

Having butterflies

Not being able to speak

Warm to the touch

Always thinking of someone

Willing to learn and grow

Making sacrifices

Compromise, Unconditional

Never ending

Breath taking

True bliss, Cool breeze

Gorgeous sunset, Sweetest smell

Trust, Honest, Loyal

Scary, Cautious

Love is...... You and I

Prayer:

"I just want to talk. I'm not sure I know how too anymore. May I start with some questions? I guess I just did......but who am I? I'm told you know everything. If you have the secret could you share it with me? I thought I knew but every day I'm challenged. You're supposed to keep me safe. I'm more exposed than ever. What's the point of death? To make us feel pain so we would forever indebted with life?

Along with that why is death not compassionate or sympathetic? Why is there no empathy or time off for death? It makes house calls and hospital visits all around the world simultaneously. No matter the age, doesn't care how tragic it has to be in order to claim it's victims. Why does there consistently have to be pain, anger, and heartache?

Why is my soul eternally and everlastingly tarnished? Because of my sins which are caused by my flesh? From not being able to make conscious decisions. Straight to only concentrating on the dumbest decisions I've ever made?

Can I be fixed? Is my view of the world the way you want me to see it? Do you still want me to have an open heart and peaceful mind? How much can I take before I brake? When I collapse will you be there? Did you make me strong enough? Is my faith strong enough in you?

If we are all your children then why do you let the children of your children suffer? Why does life suffocate you rather then breath into you? How are we supposed to acknowledge and love you when we can't even love our blood brother's and sister's? How can we learn if our teachers are just as corrupt?

I apologize for all the questions that I am asking. I know it's been a very long time. I guess the situation is really simple. I've lost my way and myself. I just need your help. Please bring me closer to you.... If that is even possible. I pray."

Mirage:

A consumption of the entity to which I called me or maybe it has no name.
Or perhaps I am just too ashamed to face it, more afraid of the power that comes with it.

Actually afraid of the power I have lost in spite of it. Visibility is just darkness yet I can see every obstacle. The air thick and dense, asphyxiation, but with new life.

Well, the life I thought I had left behind, now we walk together. Hand in hand, wait I'm just holding sand. As in precious memories that will soon be unable to evade time.

How long have I been out here. How long have I been following this self made compass? I can't seem to find where self is. Can't remember if it was myself or yourself or maybe ourselves.

The earth scorched and smokey behind my footsteps in the wake of destruction. I'm sinking, I can't move, quicksand.
I'm submerged in it I open my mouth to gasp in air one more time. Its my own blood, all of my sins.

I close my eyes, I feel my lifeless body rolling then it stops. I open my eyes no longer submerged; bruised, blistered, bones broken. The weight of guilt starts to crush my chest. My ribs crack puncturing my lungs and they collapse.

Each gasp of air I take is filled with something different. First gasp; lies. Second gasp; fear. Third gasp; disappointment. Fourth gasp; failure. Final gasp; forgiveness.

Water hits the back of my throat it sends a burning sensation throughout my entire body. My mouth puckers, acknowledging that its venom in my body not water.

My life has been filled with poison killing my own self but from within.

Packed My Bags:

I packed my bags today

Not so that I may leave and never come back

Not so that I can run away from this so called life

I packed my bags today.

Not so I can take a vacation

Not so I can go on a camping trip with my family

I packed my bags today

Not because I'm getting ready to move on with my life

or this house that I call home

I packed my bags today

Not so I could leave my daughter behind

Not so I would just be another statistic of a black father

I packed my bags today

I'm not doing this because I am afraid

I'm not wanted or being made to leave town

I packed my bags today

Not so I could kiss my loved ones goodbye

and watch the tears stream down their faces

I packed my bags today

With a promise that I will return

With a promise that I will stand for what's right

I packed my bags today

To protect the lives that we all live and for this thing we call freedom

I packed my bags today

To hold the uniforms that I am so proud to wear

To remind me of the honor it is to serve this great country

I packed my bags today

So that we may never forget 9/11

So that THEY will never forget 9/11

I packed my bags today

Because I am an United States Sailor, Marine, Soldier, Airman

I packed my bags today......

To go to war

Ownership:

"Can you pass the salt please"

       "My bitch don't pass salt, ask me nigga."

"Do you have an extra umbrella?"

       "My bitch don't use umbrellas, I wrap her in plastic, get a rain coat bruh"

"Can I use your lighter?"

       "Ask my bitch for a lighter again my nigga, and I'll burn this house down with all of us in here"

"What time..."

       "My bitch!"

"Where are we supposed......"

       "MY BITCH!"

"ACHHHHOOO"

       "Bitch you better not say bless you, #mybitch!"

Just wanted to say women are amazing, loving, caring, powerful and intelligent creatures. Created in the most beautiful image that isn't duplicated by anything else.

They aren't property.

Sun Rise:

Is that what I'm witnessing here?

Something so majestic and timeless

A start to a new day and another day to be thankful for

The dark and the storm is over

Now there is just peace and serenity

Maybe I'm getting ahead of myself

Maybe it's just me that feels

Complete

This sunrise gives me hope

And lets me know that yesterday had come and gone

But tomorrow is forever

Because tomorrow never comes.

Faith is what I am giving out

Trust is what is giving to me

Love is what I hold on too

Honesty is what I use as protection

Loyalty is what I shield the people I love with.

Does not the sunrise make you stronger

Does it not give you warmth

Show you east and west so that you're never lost

Does it not shed light on all that was dark

Everything no longer hidden

Everything and everyone accepted for who and what they truly are

Sun Rise isn't about the sun at all

It's about feeling all of these things

By simply seeing what the light touches from the sun rising.

Still to this day I can't find anything more beautiful

Then when I wake up and I see the light touching you.

She Is….

Not yet whole.
A former shell of who and what she use to be

Yet her presence is commanding
Her eyes piercing
Her voice, a deathless song

Unsure of the value she holds
.... or the value she presents
Holding characteristics of the summer solstice
A day you never want to end

Humble to a fault
Never expressing the pain she feels
Always wiling to carry the world
And everyone in it

She wears strength like a winter coat
Her tears kamikaze on her hands
In an exuberant manner
Releasing what was inside

Beauty
Unrelenting
The same as her spirit

Broken

Used

Abused

Love

Pieces of a puzzle all fitting together to be
Exactly who she is.

Beautiful.... You are:

Not just the definition of it.

Not just something that's pretty to look at it

   When I say you're beautiful baby, I mean it in a different way.

   As if I'm looking at a statuesque sunset that only God can paint

Don't get me misunderstood this ain't

Some type of way I'm trying to holler at ya

     Just want you to see the beauty that your kids see

      When they look at their mom

Knowing that she loves them no matter what

Unconditionally, willing to give your life for them never

      Forsaking them and putting on a front

      Like we don't know they are your heart

Doing everything you can for them

So they know, you guys will never be apart

    The beauty as in the loyalty that you give to your man

    Letting him know that you are there for him and you two

Will walk beside each other hand in hand

When I say you are amazingly beautiful

     I'm not looking at the color of your eyes

     I'm looking at the hope that people see in them

     Whenever you think your dreams have died

When I say, damn you sexy

Not talking about your ass in those jeans

    I'm talking about the way we connect to each other

And what having each other's backs really means.

See when I look at you and say you're beautiful

I'm not talking about your outward appearance

No... not at all

I'm talking about the things that make you who you are

I'm talking about the beauty of your soul.

We've been patiently waiting for months now, teasing, eyeing each other, day dreaming, thoughts running through our heads.

After many times of resisting and not giving in every time we are together the night comes that we just can't resist each other's touch. Every touch sends tingles and goosebumps running throughout our bodies. With sparks igniting the flame we've longed for you begin to kiss me. I take off your shirt and you take control over my body. I succumb to you and I am enslaved by your hands around my neck. My hair not in a ponytail you use it to guide me as if I'm your prized stallion. It turns me on!

You steer me to the kitchen and slam me into a chair. You pull my head back with hair in hand and kiss me. I can hardly breath as each kiss continues to make me wetter than the last. I'm dripping and throbbing my body's core temperature is rising.

As we kiss you unbutton my shirt a little and rub my breast going under my bra and pinching my nipples just ever so lightly. Then without warning my pants and panties are off. In one, what seems like effortless, motion I can feel the coldness of the chair on my thighs and butt. My vagina is seeping, running on to the chair. I watch you get on your knees you lift my legs up and spread them apart.

You dive in pressing you tongue against my clit, making my body tighten and me hold my breath. I can't help but gasp for air as you're making me moan. I grasp at your head pushing your head further into me. I can't take, I begin to start tapping out your tongue is making my body contort.

So you stop eating me, and as you get up from your knees you let your hands flow up my body grasping my breast and start kissing my neck working your way to my lips.

You grab me by my throat as we stand up, again I love it when you take control, you're kissing me and my hands work their way down your body. Into your pants I can feel your erect penis in my hands. I stop kissing you and pull your pants down. I take your penis in my mouth.
I thrust my mouth back and forth sucking and moving my tongue around. With one hand playing with your balls the other rubbing all over your chest dragging my nails as I go down. You pull away but I grab you and pull you closer. As you're enjoying yourself I move my hand down and help myself playing with my clit my whole body throbbing soaking wet wanting you.

Unable to wait any longer, I stand up and say "Take Me!" You rip my shirt off unhook my bra and throw me on the kitchen table.
You kiss and nibble on neck as you make your way up to my earlobe. You bite it then like my ear followed by a whisper "Let me love you." As your hips make their way in between my thighs

Still pleasuring me you rub your hard throbbing dick on my clit

You start teasing only putting in the tip. Watching my body react to wanting you so bad. I wrap my lip around yours biting your bottom lip.

"I'm all yours." I wrap my legs around you and drive your penis in my dripping wet vagina. Moans come from both of us.

Don't:

I don't need a special day to discover the love I have for you.

I don't need the wind at my back or an entire arsenal to show you I will always fight for you.

I don't need our song to play in order to reach your pinnacle vivacity

I don't need extreme heat to forge and shape a statue of us

I don't need a voice to always be your advocate

I don't need a clock to devote my time and attention to you

I don't need transportation in order to reach you, I'm always here

I may not need a lot. But I will always need you.

Ifocusonyou:

I- can't believe we found each other

F-ear is not an option for us we will continue to trust each other

O-ur lives have been changed for the better

C-onsistency is something we should strive for. That we never forget what we mean to each other.

U-nsettling we should always push each other to the next level

S-avor each and every second we spend with each other

O-utgoing we should always welcome new challenges and work through them together.

N-eutral and Unbiased as we travel in life side by side.

Y-early is our focus as we strive to be better as humans, lovers, friends, parents, and children than we were last year.

O-pportunistic as long as it helps better us and the people around us.

U-nanimous is what our decisions will be because we will make them together.

9/11

What does that mean to me?

It's a constant reminder of lives given, so we could all remain free.

If that's what you want to call it, my mind is being pulled in another direction. Where I suffered a great loss. As many of us have.

God allowed death to take my best friend from me. Not only my best friend but the woman who held me before either of my parents.

My lively hood, my heartbeat, my oxygen. Each day looking for answers I know she has but I can't hear her voice.

I'm so blind and so lost without her. I don't know how I can keep this up. There is no sleep only reality of the thoughts in my mind.

I'm so lost without her guidance. I have strayed from the man she wanted me to be.

Every decision I have to make, I'm looking for her approval. When my faith is shaken she would remind me how much I'm loved.

She can hear me I know she can, she has too.

I have to tell her about the things happening in my life, but I'm too afraid to visit her final resting place.

Because in my mind....

She still exists!

My grandma

Me:

I don't know what to say
I don't know what to do
I chose modesty
In confusion with honesty
I found you
A new gateway...
If you would,
Trying to love me
Understand me
As I grow into manhood
But I didn't care for you
Not like I should
My mistakes amplified
Not running to you
And always over analyzed
Looking at your face
Wanting to touch you
So tormented in this place
Always hurting you
Never wanted us to not be
Just wasn't sure if you could continuously
Love the imperfection of simply
Just being me

Dear Daughter:

I wanted to write you a letter.

But thought a poem would be better.

A letter would be words linked together in order to paraphrase.

A poem would allow emotions that I can't subjugate.

I'm getting ahead of myself...well more like off track.

I stay awake watching you, wondering, and protecting you: insomniac.

Let me say what I need to say in order for you to appreciate the love, our bond we have no one can brake.

Today is your birthday and I'm just astounded.

Full of life, joy, love and a mind completely unbounded.

Beauty of a little girl that is incomprehensible.

Drive me in multiple directions with in; becoming inspirational

Then I truly exceed not only my potential, but also my dreams.

Viewing through the lens of your soul that steadily shines: agleam.

In a world filled with disgust and anguish we stand divided.

But you are love of the future.

I just have to make sure you're not misguided.

Never thought so much of you, would be the reflection of myself.

I admire and envy your innocence, along with the vow to protect it until my last breath.

I, the perfect teacher and father figure.

Having you a part of my life, now a student: transfigured.

Christmas?!?

The meaning behind Christmas.

What is it?

A day to celebrate the birth of Jesus?

A day to celebrate St. Nick?

The day we exchange gifts to one another?

Where love is shared throughout family and friends?

Eating your favorite entrees, sides, and

deserts?

Decorations and carolers igniting the holiday cheer?

Christmas....

What if your faith is shaken in God or you don't believe?

What if St. Nick forgets about you?

How about your alone on Christmas day without loved to be shared?

What if you don't have food to eat?

What if you don't have a place to sleep?

And holiday cheer doesn't seem to extend its hand out to you?

Christmas.....

So this year think about your meaning of Christmas and then think about what Christmas means to those around you.

Not just your home, but your neighborhood, your community, your city.

Merry Christmas

Help Wanted:

Major repairs needed.

Here's a list of what's broken.

Trust:

She must believe and know that you will keep your word and always be there no matter what.

Honesty:

Tell her and show her that you have nothing to hide and that your heart is true, and 100% hers.

Loyalty:

Must maintain and be committed only to her. Make her know and feel that she is number one, the only one. Don't make your job top priority.

Compassion:

Be considerate and accepting to her needs. Whatever it is whether its holding her, listing, spending a little time with her. Just do it. It will pay off in the end.

Honor:

Take pride that she wants, and loves just you. Defend her, fight for her, show her that you truly are blessed to have her. She needs, wants, and deserves it.

Love:

She should never ever doubt that you love her and are in love with more than life its self. Day in and day out.

Tools Needed:

A Broom:

To sweep up the pieces of her heart that was shattered.

A Box:

To put those pieces in

Tape and Glue:

To put these pieces of her heart back together.

If you feel like you meet all the requirements please submit your application. I will call you and set up an interview, because its my job you will be taking

Hate:

When I say I hate you I truly do but I think there is a misconception about it. You see; I say I hate you but truly I just hate myself.

I hate the fact that I don't know who I am anymore. The fact that every thought I have is a picture of you. I can't remember the last time I thought about putting myself first.

Now I wish I had.

I hate you so much but hate myself more. I look in the mirror and I don't know who the person starring back at me is.

My face once pretty is now different colors and swollen. My back was straight with confidence and strength. Now I'm huddled over in fear and disgust.

You call my name my skin crawls, you tell me you love me and my stomach churns. I walk constantly looking at the ground. I no longer have the courage to face anyone.

I'm alone in this hell. Alienated from all friends and family I loved you too much, I was too blind.

I thought you accepted me for me not for your work horse that I've become. I can't find an escape. The drugs don't do it and the liquor makes it worse.

I'm ready for the pain and paranoia to end. No longer will I wonder if people see me or see my scars.

I hate you but hate myself more.
No longer will I live with hate
No longer living in fear.
No longer ......
Living at all.

Mysterious:

Isn't Life? The way life starts, the way life becomes of value, with its ever changing views.

Not only life, but love

Or maybe we are looking at life and love all wrong.

Is it possible that maybe life and love are actually the same. One simply doesn't exist without the other.

Even in the midst of all the chaos our lives bring. Within each moment we can find an example or the presence of love.

We celebrate special days and events that bring us together as friends, family, and the human race.

Banding together right after tragedy strikes remembering the lives taken, but never forgetting the love that never leaves.

The crashing into people and objects just to feel...no, be closer.

The smile of a stranger, or the laugh of a baby, the smell of puppy's breath. All these things that represent life and endlessly bestow love.

LIFE!

That is you, that is what I have been able to see in you, it is the greatest gift I've ever been allowed to receive.

I've often wondered about these mysterious things called life and love. Especially when in your presence.

I now know it is life, and life is filled with love, and that your life is love, and in that you give life, in the love you give. I'm honored to have been found by that love and to have this life.

Fighting:

       I think I've given up the will to fight. Always starting from the very bottom trying to escape quickly so that the hope isn't beating out of me. Am I fighting? Can I truly say I am? If so what is it I'm fighting for, or possibly against.

With things like faith and belief set for a head on collision with fact and science. Keep me questioning "what is it I believe in."

Could I possibly be fighting for someone. People that love me or people I'm in love with.
Am I fighting with them or against them.

The fight is a physical one, no an emotional one where it twist the soul and conquers the heart: it's physical my back is against the wall....
Time is the enemy.

Not enough hours in the day to continue the fight. To push on, not enough energy to hold my fist up. To defeated to swing.

Fight the words, include the feeling in them but toss aside the meaning. What is the very meaning anyway. We fight to get to it, but are always too sensitive to accept it.

It's the constant fight on the job. The lack of compassion on the job. Treated like a number, because we fought for equality. Now we aren't even human.

It's the test in faith. The belief in the Almighty. Then the disbelief when your world crumbles around you. Or is it a new beginning? Has the dirt been brushed off? No I'm still on the ground...right?

I give up. I'm tired of fighting for....or against.....
Well damn...I don't know any more.

Congratulations:

Congratulations to the mother to be, as time goes on and the days are way to long I'm sure you'll see. That the life you are creating will be a great one. While you are waiting to meet the first unconditional real true love of your life.

Remember to savor each and every moment. Remember the first look, the first smile. The first time he holds your hand. The first time he calls you mom. The first time he cries out for you and you make him all better. Remember the first moment you will be proud of him. Remember the first time you'll be disappointed in him, but then help lift him back up. Remember the undeniable bond that you two share because you carried him.

Remember the love that you have for him and also understand that no woman will ever, be ever to match it. Remember the times he annoys the crap out of you. Remember the first time he pees on you. Remember the way his face makes your day better. Remember how the sound of his laugh lights up your world.

Remember all the tears yet to be cried and all of the pain yet to be had. But it will be worth it and he will be grateful. Because there is no love greater than that of a mother's. So again congratulations to a woman who's heart has just been completely opened and who's beauty will never be matched in his eyes.

Congratulations to a boy who will have everything he could possibly ever need and want.....
You as a mother

Just woke up, my eyes are trying to focus. I turn my head and there on pillow, right next to me.

Is the understatement of my life that describes pure extasy.

Her eyes aren't open yet so I study her. As in to watch her so carefully I'm in complete disbelief.

That I was chosen. I can't figure out for the life in me,

On how her selection process went. But here I am and there she is

I lean in closer and carefully so I don't disturb her slumber.

I touch her, brush her hair back just enough so I can acknowledge heaven is truly on earth.

In its most rarest and creative forms. I push my lips against hers and the power is too much.

I move back and lift my hand in the air trying to clutch

The new life I have been blessed with. Just then her eyes open....I can't move I'm paralyzed.

She says "Good morning, baby". Then it hits me. I have been blessed with the greatest reality that is you.

The Girl:

Ahhh yes there she is.

A nervous disposition to what could be, and what is.

The ever present adolescence of my beating heart.

Unprepared for the beautiful journey I must embark

Written for and by love, life's greatest script

An unmistakable quiver in my lips.

As I search for words that never appear.

My presence in front of her is just austere.

A flash of a smile that causes me to lose direction.

Eye contact which manifests undeniable affection.

The simplest touch between our hands.

Set forth in motion a divine plan.

Displaying souls so effervescent.

Integrated without protest; acquiescent

I the boy, she the girl

Find ourselves in one another's world.

A masterpiece of passionate contrivance.

Two hearts that find acceptance.

High emotions have been obtained.

In response to unconditional love that sustains.

For this is a love not built remised

Just forged inevitably by fate and the first kiss.

The place where your heart is. What happens if it's a fear you know all to well because it's where the darkness lives. The darkness inside of you.

Where your mother isn't doing as well as you thought she was and you just continue to fight and hold your head up high. The place where your father lives and presents a love so great for God, it almost makes you question your own faith.

Where past meets present and future seems lost in a never ending spiral of grief, pain and disappear. What's next after you don't know how to rebuild your relationship with your siblings. When you are so confused on what to say and who to say it too.

You find out that you just got a new brother and have inherited four more children through love. Pushing and pulling trying to put the pieces together to make sure you don't fuck up. Worried that you aren't good enough to lead this family. That you aren't man enough to accept responsibility and guidance needed to survive.

You have to do all of this without the friendly help of the bottle you so desperately crave. The one that makes reality and illusion, and illusions into dreams. Ever so strategically one burden is placed on your back one after another. Then you fall to your knees. Helpless and you can't breathe, you call out. You awake.

To find that God has sent you three God fearing women and one of them to be by your side forever. To be a helper and care giver to the children when you aren't able. To love you unconditionally no matter your mistakes and your past. To smile and lift you up from well that you have been in for so long.

The cold wet darkness has harbored you as if you were in the womb. Only for God to send you his blessing in the act of love. A love you never knew existed, something you've never felt before. Then with arms wrapped around you tight the words "everything is alright" never made more sense.

In their eyes you see the love, passion, everlasting undying love they have for God and yourself. A feeling of comfort and reassurance grows over you. Your heart fills with some type of unidentified emotion, which makes your face react...turning you lips upward and tears in your eyes.

Joy is what the emotion is called and even in a time like this you look around and can't help to say....I'm home.

Flower

I walk the same way I've always walked to work, and each and everyday I pass by this flower.

At first I never noticed but it caught my eye one day in the pouring rain.

It was raining so hard and I didn't have an umbrella so I was beaten down by this storm and yet this flower stood.

The next day I was anxious to see the flower again.

As I was approaching the flower another person in front of me stepped on it.

I looked at the flower as it laid there and felt helpless.

I just went on to work.

At work it was all I thought about and I had to check on it when I got off.

To my surprise there stood the flower, taller, stronger, and more vibrant then before.

I developed an admiration for this flower.

Each and everyday I passed it, I notice something else different about it.

I don't know how many days weeks or years I have not noticed this flower but every since I have.

It's like the flower breathed life into me.

From that faithful day of rain pouring down on me physically, and spiritually, I now know why I have to fight.

I now know why I have to keep faith and continue to love unconditionally.

I would just like to say thank you and also apologize for never acknowledging that you were my flower.

PHASE:

I can't think about anything other than you. I don't know why, maybe it's time I stop asking or trying to figure it out.. Thinking about the noises that surround us.

I look at you, you stare back at me. My head reacts to the crashing and smashing around us, yet nothing phases you. I'm afraid, I'm depleted, I'm weak, I'm tour, I'm scarred, I'm a shell of the version of me you've never seen, yet nothing phases you.

My cognizance of self far out ways the perception and vision of co habitation. Future bleeds out, my past plays on repeat, my present is just the very idea of existing, yet nothing phases you.

I let words drip from my tongue slowly as to provide a nectar of spiritual serene. I let my hands form a cascade on your skin, suggest you are life. I let my eyes fill with acceptance and a language only they can speak, yet nothing phases you.

Nothing phases you.

You always focus and see me.

His Menu:

I come over to the house you cooked dinner. But I'm not hungry for any of the food you cooked. You open the door I come in, you close the door behind me. Then you turn around look up, just to find that it's too late! My hand is around your neck and I slam you up against the door.

I move one of my hands from your waist and pull down the collar of your shirt. My other hand from your neck to your hair. I pull your head to the side and sink my teeth into your neck.
I retract, then sink my teeth into your neck and collar bone.
I retract and then sink my teeth into your shoulder.

I let go of your shirt I kiss your lips and then I put my hands in your pants. Reaching your panties.
I stay on the outside of them and keep moving downward until I get to your pussy.

I start rubbing your clit feeling wetness through your panties.
I grabbed you by the hair and lead you to the couch.
I pull your pants down bend you over.

I smack your ass and grab it. Pull your hair some more. I get on my knees. I spread your legs a little and then I put my tongue on your pussy.
On the clit, your lips, and in your hole.
Going over your asshole just a little

I smack your ass a couple times while my tongue is in you.
I stop eating, get off my knees pull you up by your hair.

I turn you around so that you face me and then I kiss you putting my tongue in your mouth so you can taste your own pussy.
Then I take off you shirt and bra.

You rip my clothes off of me I throw you down on the couch. I put my hard cock in your mouth. It gives me so much pleasure.

You suck on it take your tongue and lick the tip. Then you take my cock and deep throat it, making my shaft completely disappear in your mouth. My senses over load and I'm about to cum.

I pull away and move down I push your titties around my cock and begin to titty fuck you. While I'm doing this you bend your head down and open your mouth.

As I stroke up with your titties surrounding my cock, the tip makes its way into your mouth just enough for you to suck on it for a second. I pull it back and stroke up again, and repeat. I can't take it anymore! I explode on the last stroke my body is barely able to handle. You never release from your mouth as I tremble.

Our hearts are beating fast as we both give in to each other and the temptation of our bodies crying out for each other. I move down, nibble and suck on your nipples. Our pheromones mix together and create an aroma of desire, lust, passion, and ecstasy.

We are breathing in sync my cock rock hard and your pussy flooding the sheets.

I position myself and I slide right in.

I pull out and then slowly push in.

I pull out and then push it in as deep as I can go.

Your back arches you grab the sheets I grab your waist and pull you towards me. Neither one of us breathing, just frozen in that moment.

Been thinking:

About what you ask.

The complexity of my face that you think is just a mask.

The sound of my heart that hits like the bass

and my voice the snare.

Caught up in this endless chase called love as the sun creates a glare.

So powerful and relentless

I can't do anything but close my eyes.

Left feeling defenseless in the discovery of you...a surprise.

In the wake of not finding my voice.

Your eyes pierce deep into my soul.

I wish I could rejoice, and just let everything go.

Instead I stand the most vulnerable and out of control.

Going with a strong, uncomfortable non changing mindset.

That I can love and accept love

without any regrets.

Just a battle with in me

And you are at the center.

You have brought a very plentiful spring.

In my darkest, coldest and loneliest of Decembers.....

It's what I've been thinking about

All the time, never ending, day and day out.

Shadows:

Casting out various shapes and forms to provoke a reaction.

Movements flowing effortlessly, consuming all light in its path.

Reaching and surpassing what was thought to be impossible, is only now inevitable.

Fear accompanies abandoned hearts and self imprisoned minds.

The faint smell of the most recent lives that have been claimed.

A trail of tears and blood left by the ones still running.

I with pen and paper.
Unwillingly spared to keep alive its hunger.

Shadows taken shape of the past.

Confusion:

Feeling confused about the way this works I try to do everything the way you want me to but I keep falling short.

At some point I realize that it's not me that's falling short. It's the fact that every goal I achieve you set the next one higher. I'm starting to realize that the bar you have set is intangible.

I can't reach it nor will I ever. It's simply because you cannot reach your goals that someone else has set for you.

You fall short I fall short, we both continue to spiral on a path the never satisfies the people that hold our bars and ourselves.

Waking up every day just to continue striving in a fairytale world.

Working to hard to see the inevitable end that sits right next to us. Domino's in this game of life falling on top of each other to gain success.

Or is it the illusion of success? I want to be what you want me to be so much and yet I despise the very thought of it daily. I receive mixed signals, traffic lights with a stop sign in the middle surrounded by green.

 Always being afraid to put my best foot forward, neither are good enough.

Underestimating the power of love that leads me so blindly.

Giving to much credit to my own mind which hasn't fully awaken yet, if at all. Mistaken the darkness for light.

Spectators:

Good morning!

Spectators, assumers, non believer's, non supporters. Today is the day that I appreciate you even more. Without you my flame would have never been ignited. I feel better then ever taking into account letting my family and friends see the real me.

Not with a bottle attached to my hand but with learning how to appreciate life and all it brings. I held my lil nephew, which apparently automatically makes him my son based on the picture that is on Facebook.

My call list is getting shorter and shorter only letting in the people who I need to let in. Friends and girlfriends come and go but I can't change two things: my blood and my past. You turn over a material possession with your trust to a woman who despises you. This worldly possession was supposed to be returned.

Now you look like the fool! Spectators just sit watch then write their own story. Always using the word "allegedly" with no proof of anything other then what they believe. You sit and are supposed to have my back where you secretly wish for me to fail. The truth of the matter is while you are in the stands I am on the field. Not just any other field I'm on the battlefield. Within myself, fatherhood, military, friendship, and life period.

I will continue to use my talents and play to the best of my ability while you decide to join my team or stay in the stands. This choice is not mine to be made I will continue to push however, I just need to know where you will stand.

So I can't decide whether to grab your hand or move around you.

<h1 style="text-align:center">The Product:</h1>

I guess you could call me that The representation of two lives united Dark complexion, hair braided, depicted of deep African roots...

Also known as black

A mother born up north in the 40's Struggling to get by

And a father born in the 50's down south

Always fighting for his life
Born in the land of the free Due to the color of my skin
I'm always indebted

No record on file

No current or prior convictions

The world is in denial Secretly praying, for self execution
Not acknowledging any of my beliefs or character and the fact I'm a veteran

I kneel, it's not the time
We kneel, now we're suspects of a crime
You kneel and a life is lost
They kneel in protest "we understand the cost"

I am the Product

Raised in suburbia

Father worked in a factory

Not one complaint

Impervious
To keep grasp of the family
Mother gave her heart in soul
Using unconditional
love thankfully
In my eyes she raised me right
My perspective
Shouldn't matter that I'm white.

I treated the world with respect
Not an attitude of "I'm better than..."
I still drew regret
It didn't matter that I was a veteran.

No where to sleep
Park benches became my home
No place of retreat
From the countless dreams
Heaume

My time on this earth
Has come to an end
Blame placed since birth
Beaten to death
As I closed my eyes to rest
 Due to the color of my skin.

I am the Product.

We are all The Products of our environment.
All black people are not threats
All white people are not evil

We should stand united and create a new environment so that our children become better products.

I'm not.....:

The kind of man who makes promises.

The kind of man who doesn't take care of his family.

The man who is cheating and lying in life.

A man who doesn't support the people who he loves.

A man who is haunted and hunted by his past

A sanctimonious or self righteous man

The man who's back has weakened by the load he carriers

A fearful man

A man of disbelief and dishonor

The man who's loyalty is questioned

The man......

I'm not the man I want to be

I'm living in a illusion

The truth is I am everything listed above with more faults.

However today is the day I stand up and say.

I'm not another man.

I'm my own Man

And I will stay true to who I am as I'm on this journey to become the man I want to be.

Guys:

What happened today?
I guess I could tell you.

You won't judge me or complicate this relationship, will you?

Tell me you love me then pull back so hard on my heart string I instantly become your yoyo.

Doing tricks trying to accommodate the way you feel, letting myself slip away so that I may keep you.

For what though I'm running out of reasons for the reasoning of being in love.

Lost in an abyss of emotional abandonment reaching out for a hand to help me.

I'm flailing around frantic, gasping for air and being suffocated by need for you to notice me. I have placed you above everything. Even the air I need to breath.

My world has evolved to become yours. Just take a second look at me, see the love in my eyes. Feel my chest and how my heart pumps my body with life, that you bring.

Watch my world completely stop spinning every time you're near.

Or will you accept me as your "cliche" night in shinning armor. Defensively fighting and surviving for the universes greatest honor to hold....your love.

I'm sorry I got side tracked.

You ask me what happened today?
Oh......
She said
"Hi!"

Shell:

Silence or noise I don't know which one I prefer due to the never ending circum-
stances that surround me.

Just lost in what is supposed to be faith but my beliefs don't have a foundation.

I'm spinning, Just spinning I have become the vortex.

Or maybe not the vortex rather a figment of everything that is. I'm searching for
self within self.

I inhale or am I exhaling. Breathing is no longer simple but so complex that my
lungs have adjusted to the lack of a continuous need for oxygen.

I'm not suffering; I don't think I am. Numb to pain numb to happiness numb to
my thoughts.

I've been here for so long.
It's my protection from the world.

My protection from myself.
Here from within

Here inside...

The shell.

Broken:

I am.....

Trustworthy

Filled with love

I've tried to be understanding

Always here when you need me

Never judgmental

Taking risk every day to expose myself and my soul to you

Never questioning how I feel for you

Feeling completely melted

Out of control

Now wondering who I am

No

Wondering who you are

Giving so free so on top of the world

Crying alone

Asking y aren't you here

But you.....

Y do you Only care about yourself

Filled me with your lies

Made me the fool

Gave me false hopes

With broken promises

I thought for so long I was broken...

Then I realized......

I have never been broken.

I just allowed people in my life who needed me to fix them.

Waiting:

For any tall tale sign of a clearer night, or a love that was so pure and
so flawless even the diamonds in the sky were jealous.

What happens if you've waited but never grasp the substantial
and yet potent heart of all hearts.

What if there is a love that gets caught just like a common cold?

Where two people are destined to be in each others lives as one soul.

Not soul mates, but rather inhabitants and ever present in your daily routine. Then
what? Your heart beats fast, your temperature rises, and life completely changes.

What you thought you needed is now only a memory and
what you wanted is now considered a joke.

Before you lies the greatest thing you've ever encountered. Your one true love.

Taking you by surprise as most of them do. Whether it's in driver's ed class,
brief encounter at a store, or the wonderful world of Facebook.

The connection is undeniably the one thing you've longed for but never knew it.

True love does exist

It's not what you think.

It's being there all the time no matter what and at any time always
given up yourself for their needs.

It's countless days of uplifting, encouragement, honesty, and faith.

It's undying, everlasting, selflessness.

It's being stunned by a beauty you know only God can create. It's hearing
a voice that sounds like it's straight from heaven. It's seeing a picture
and begin reminded how great love is.

This is why I believe life is so great.

We are all looking for something more when in reality we are only waiting on love.

Combination:

You are the right combination.

Or should I say the best.

The classic beauty of Marilyn Monroe or any pin up doll.

With the fire and loyalty of Bonnie.

A tough exterior that says I don't take shit from anyone. Matched with a heart that says I'll give you all I can.

The capability to hang with the boys. But the tender touch of still being a lady.

The sturdy hand and strict voice of a father. Matched by the understanding and compromise of a mother.

The independence to conquer the world, and the humility to ask for help when needed.

The strength to carry any burden no matter the weight, and then will assist in helping carrying a friend.

Being everything and everyone, provider, banker, lawyer, doctor, mother, father, queen, and a friend.

It was made clear to me....

And I agree. That you are the perfect combination.

Power of Love:

If I was a blind man my hands would never stop touching you.

If I was a deaf man sign language would not be able to translate your beauty.

If I was wheelchair bound I'd run just to be next to you.

If my lungs collapsed your voice would be my oxygen.

World:

You're my sunshine

You're my warmth

You're my sunrise and my sunset

You're the glow of the moon and the shimmering of the stars

You're the wind that gently touches my face

You're all four seasons keeping me on my toes and always taking my breath with beauty

You are my world

That's what I'm here for:

To be there when you need me.

To inspire you and believe

In your dreams

That's what I'm here for

To help you achieve and accomplish your goals.

All the while providing you with a partner or life coach that we all so desperately crave.

Someone in our lives that can help save

Us from ourselves.

That's what I'm here for

Not to be afraid of what our love doesn't offer

 but to literally be a buffer for what our love does provide.

As we take each others hand in stride and create a reach that's well beyond the stars.

Stroking on the strings of my guitar, which is also known as my heart.

As we impart, finally to the rest of the world. That I support you, and also adore.

I keep telling you

This is what I'm here for.

Thankless:

I am broken and completely depleted of moral self.

I stand here as you send your words out like drones engaging a target.

And a face that has never seen real misfortune.

On my way home cars honk their horns and flip me off.

Kids walk out in the middle of the street and look at me like I'm the moron as I slam on the breaks and my tires screech.

A couple of cops parked outside the gas station watch me walk in. I open the door for an older woman and watch her clinch her purse tighter as she passes me.

All this for 30 minutes...30 minutes is what I get.

Back in the car back to being held accountable for other people's actions and my own.

More words are launched at me.

More uncontrolled and thoughtless orders are given to me.

I'm looked at and treated as if the freedom everyone has isn't paid for.

Didn't I sacrifice, didn't I pay, didn't I carry the burden of maintaining your freedom?

I gave my all to the military for protection of this great land.

Only to return a black, homeless, overworked, underpaid, mentally messed up, loss of self, alcoholic.

All because I use to believe in something great.

Not the nation, but the people of this great nation.

Here I stand confused, angry, and thankless!

Fairytale:

I use to think that fairytales where just for children.

I never knew what it truly meant for people to say "the sun will come out tomorrow." I didn't know that life would throw me so many curveballs and through so many storms.

Happy endings never seemed to find me. Always looking for a way to fit in and not be so different....

But I have a better purpose in life and I now know that fairytales are real....

Because I found you

I found out that I'm not a freak looking to fit in.

Instead a man who you would give a chance too. In the past couple weeks you have shown me that honesty, compassion, understanding, and forgiveness are key.... also misunderstandings too.

Set into a trance by your beauty, heaven on earth could never be better.

My days are filled with new life and I a new me.

Telling the world that I mean something to someone and she gives me reasons to move forward.

You are my fairytale.

Love is also....

Torture

Madness

Painful

Stomach tying knots

Broken trust

Argumentative Lies

Heartache

Nights at the bar

Trust in God

Lost of faith

Self deprivation

Never being good enough

Settlement

Judgment

Lost in translation

Spiteful

Jealousy

Blind

Love is also.....

E.V.O.L

Risk:

Is taking a moment to not understand your surroundings or the people you are with.

Instead of understanding you simply accept what is in front of you. You let go of doubt and fear. You stand at the edge of the cliff before you jump.

Your heart races and then without remorse or a glance back your feet leave the ground.

You're in the air all the laws of gravity do not apply to you. Complete and total freedom.

Until you start to fall. Now all of a sudden you start to think about things like "was it worth it".

Should I have been so careless....

Look at your husband or wife
Look at your children
Look at the friends you have made over the past years.
Look in the mirror.....

Now ask yourself....haven't you been worth the risk.

I think you underestimate yourself

It's not a curse just the fact

You are goal oriented and so are the men you want to be with

You are drawn to men who want to be successful

Have a good head on their shoulders

Alot of that comes with risk

You aren't horrible

You are actually amazing

It was just hard to sit and watch you be hurt

Afraid to live your life

So I moved on with mine

Was it right

Did it hurt you

Of course

I just thought you would never

Be ready to leave and be with me

You're very intelligent

Your heart is so big.

The love you have to give

Greater than anyone could imagine

You are your own woman now

Not really influenced by whatever newcomer comes alone.

I like your confidence you have now

It's beautiful

So are you

Inside and out

Starting Over:

From square one dealing with who you are and who I am.

Juggling the substance of what our lives are made up of

Or maybe it's that we are still trying to find out exactly what it is.

Trying to find the balance between you, me, us, and them but yet we are too near sited to see we can't even plan for tomorrow

We can't even plan for the next hour

That's what we are agreeing to right.

To live a life where we pass each other in passing

We aren't torn apart by our past instead they have consumed us

As we both lie and say that it has no barring on us.

Every time we look up its like we are just glancing in the rear view mirror on the place we are trying to leave

What's ironic about that is the fact we have yet to stick the key in the ignition to even start to drive away

Both set in our on ways watching the world around us spin and we wrap ourselves in the only thing we know and accept: time

Our foundation is built on false hopes and unstable faith

We just focus on ourselves and avoid the one thing we a truly afraid of

The need and want to be needed and wanted the silver lining is we can't let anyone in

So what should we do

Tear each other down rip up the foundation that we call "ourselves" and deconstruct the world as we know it...

....sigh....

Staying the same is hard

Starting over is even harder

Words I Couldn't Say:

How long has it been?
Minutes?
Hours?
Day's?
Seems like year's
Maybe it hasn't been that long.

But since you haven't been here
I'm no longer time conscious
Every beat of my heart echos
In the vast emptiness
Which at one point use to be me.

You left and took me with you
You left but are still here.

Wondering if I'll ever hold you again.
Waiting to hear you say
I love you
Looking to gaze in your spell casting eyes.

Listening to hear the Angels sing.

I think you call it your voice.

Looking for the love I once had.

Now lost and encrypted like binary code.
Happiness eludes me as if it's performing magic tricks.

My mind forever imprinted with memories of you.

How you provide the sweetest nectar I've ever tasted.

My arms use to swaddle your skin.

The look of complete joy as my lips uttered the words.
Babygirl.

All of these things I over looked.

Never letting you hear my heart.

That only beats for you.

Not acknowledging that you are the only song I want to hear.

The only love I ever knew.

Do you remember?

Remember our love?
Of course you don't.
Because our love was filled.
With words I couldn't say.

Making Love:

Here you and I stand, anxious and afraid. Hearts racing, we step towards each other. Taking in each others scent. You have the sweetest smell I put my face in your neck and breath in. I lightly kiss your neck.

I hold you tight in my arms and I squeeze you. You squeeze me. I take a step back. I take off my shirt. You look at me cautiously and hesitate pulling your shirt half way up. Then you pull it back down. I step closer to you and I say "I love you, and nothing can change that. I love you for who you are and not what you look like". I take a step back you pause for a moment and then take off your shirt.

I look at you with complete love and non judgmental eyes. Then I take my pants off I stand in front of you only in boxers and socks. You take off your pants and immediately try to hide this beautiful temple with your arms and hands. I take the attention off of you by throwing my boxers at you. I stand naked, exposed, and vulnerable to you.

You can see all of my scars, pain, everything I have been so afraid to let you see. Finally before you just stands a man....just stands me. I'm not perfect in anyway. I don't have a six pack, I'm not extremely muscular, nor am I "in shape."

I may BE a shape, but not in shape. You look at me and study me. Take a couple of breaths, and then take off your bra. Slowly and some what reluctantly. Lower to the floor it falls. I can see your breast nothing to be ashamed of.

I see them as two uniquely crafted gifts that God designed himself, and since they are on you. They are perfect. I look directly into your eyes and tell you "I'm so in love with you". You respond "I love you more". Then you pull your panties off. We stare at each other for a moment.

Two separate souls forced into the same position due to love. We step closer, I gently caress your body with my hands you do the same. We take our time, looking into each others eyes and touching each and every scar, stretch mark, mole and any other imperfections.

Kissing every single one we find. I kiss your lips and pull your body closer to mine we are skin to skin. I take in your scent again, and truly learn to appreciate the term "Heaven on Earth". We kiss as my hand holds your face we fall back on to the bed. My hands all over your body touching you in a way you've never felt before.

I stop and sit up as I lay on you, fingers running through your hair. Neither of us say a word we just look into each others eyes. Our heartbeats have become one. We are no longer anxious, cautious, or afraid. We are simply in love, as we make love.

WDYW:

I'm trying to understand.

Understand the man

That you think I can

Become or am I

The man you want

Or you believe that you have.

Or maybe you just want me as a friend.

Whatever that means.

As of lately it seems like it depends

On the time of the day or when I'm inserted into your dreams.

The time we have is never under appreciated.

I care to much we aren't even on the same level.

That's what has been over exaggerated....

I mean repeated to me.

For me to take a step back and pretend I don't care about you.

Knowing damn well my world revolves around you.

Tell me you can see me

Tell me you want it to be me

Every day back and forth

This game of tennis

Trying to show you yourself worth

I sound like a genius

But I can't figure you out

Looking for myself to find my place

Confusion stacked up next to doubt

Mind lost in an empty space.

I just need you to tell me

What you need

And want from me

What do you want to do with us

Caught a case of the feelings

Now I'm riding on this bus
All through town in search for the healing.
I know you can provide.
The only thing is.....I
Can't stop thinking about you
Wrapping my head around a particular noise....your voice
And finding hard to even eat without you.
All of this and at times I'm sure I don't even exist
To you.
I'm begging and pleading
What do you want?
From me...

Collision:

Isn't it crazy how two world's can collide.

Both traveling at the speed of light uncontrollably.

Not knowing the course they are set on.

Or maybe it isn't two world's colliding. Rather one coming to a screeching halt stunned by a beauty unlike any other.

Perhaps it's the sweet smell of heaven on earth when you walk past her.

Could it be while in her embrace time stands still.

How every picture you see of her feels like you never see her enough.

I think it's crazy how two world's collide or maybe it's the fact that I just want to be part of yours.

Sleeping:

Thinking about how it feels to fall asleep with you in my arms...

The most calming and satisfying thing I can ever imagine.

You fall asleep on me. There's no snoring. You just drift away. Your body completely becomes heavy and feels like it's melting into mine.

Your heart beat is in perfect sync with mine. Your breathing slows down you subconsciously move in closer as if you want my arms to wrap around you twice.

I kiss your forehead softly and you smile just a little. Your hand and head on my chest. As you breath out I breath you in.

In that moment I in take your whole day. All of the stress, the noise, the disappointments, the anger and eagerness.

Right then and there we are the only two people who exist. Falling asleep with you in my arms makes me feel like I am the last man on earth.

Please:

Can you teach me
How to love
To accept love
To send love like shrapnel from a grenade
Can you teach me to be strong
Tell me where strength comes from
How to gather it
Do I use it all the time
Teach me what strength really is
Help me to understand
Understand self
Understand others
With understanding
Teach me acceptance
Accept the world around me
Accept all that I am
Accept the journey
Accept the path I'm on now
Please
Do I listen to my heart
Or my mind
Teach me to tell the difference between
Teach me
Please
How to pray
How to give comfort
How to grieve
How to overcome
How to follow
How to lead
Please teach me
How do I maintain faith
How do I maintain family
Teach me
Please

I Get High:

I know you see the title and think you can relate. But truth be told you can't even see me.

How high am I...let me articulate.
I'm on the highest of highs no drug can come close too.
Well maybe alcohol.....no that even won't do.

So you're probably thinking that I'm on some self righteous containment shit when truth be told I'm just on myself preservation shit.

Meaning I'm teaching my son's how to be men. Verses how to be the regular statistic. Meaning I'm encouraging them to be more than what meets the eye, and a little more uncommon.

I get high on showing my daughter's the blueprint of what a good man should be.

He works to provide and not just the money aspect or the material things. He provides time. What use is it seeing your children on the other side of the glass, or playing in the yard with someone who isn't you?

I get high on trying to set the example on what it is to be a man in today's society. Not judged by the color of my skin.
Nor if I'm straight, gay, single parent, or what my faith is.

No I'm bigger than that!
My dreams are no longer dreams but goals. My goals have become reality and my reality is blessed.

My high exist when my children are just as if not more successful then me.

My high comes from being a great friend, boyfriend, husband, lover, father and a man.

So when I say I get high it's simply because I'm high on keeping my last name alive and associated with the best in everything that is going on in the world.

When I say I'm looking for self preservation....that's an understatement. I'm looking for my family to be a dynasty.

That's what gets me high.

They Said:

They said that since I was born black and a male I would have two strikes against me
I guess they underestimated the strength and the faith of my father

They said that all men are created equal
I guess they haven't seen the look in someone's eyes when a person of Arabic descent boarded the plane after 9/11

They said all women are beautiful in their own way
As every cover of a magazine for over 40 years has been some respectable "model"

They said that children would be our future
Meanwhile forgetting about the parents and not allowing them to raise children properly

They said the government is out for your best interest
Really confused about that. Washington shuts down for 15 days, while factories and jobs across America are being shut down or out sourced to other countries.

They said the best things in life are free.
Hmm.......sorry I was trying to figure out the last time I got something for free

They said always be yourself
Nigger, Wetback, Jew, Chink, Cracker, Alien, Loner, Weirdo, Geek, Stupid, Whore, Dyke, Ugly, Freak, Fat, Weak, Anorexic, Cunt, Bitch, Fag, Retard.......

It seems to me that whatever it is "THEY" have said to me.
I will and have always been better then THEY

Doubles:

Is what I see

Waking up every morning

Not knowing what or who to expect

Fueled by your jealousy for me

And yet swept off your feet from others

Trust that you say is there

But if I'm not then the trust

Disappears along with your word

Held by a double standard

That only you can produce

I would say something

However, what's the use

Engaged in what can be mistaken

For a relationship

Now the hands of time

Show me that I have been

Mislead into a world

That only benefits you

Compliments, giggles, and fire

Set the tone

For your day

Which I find odd

I can never get as much time as they

Socialist in a way that can only be described

As if it's their only life line

How I wish you wouldn't subcom

Well the other you

Or maybe it's me

Maybe I refuse to double

My standards, my time, my sanity

When I look in the mirror

I only see me
I fear when you look in the mirror
You are faced with choosing
Who you have to be

Explain Alternate:

When you see him, what happens?

Does time fight against you?

Do you yearn to be closer?

Does the air become thick and opaque?

When he touches you what do you feel?

Does ever hair on the back of your neck stand?

Do goosebumps flood your entire body like a broken levee?

When he kisses you, do your taste buds rejoice?

Does your heart stop with each kiss reviving yourself as he pulls away?

When he looks into your eyes, does love reflect in them?

Is it a glimpse of the future, or is it destiny?

Has it been written?

When he makes love to you, are you transcended?

Do you completely give him everything?

As your bodies completely inelastically collide....is that where you want to stay forever?

When he says "I love you" does it touch every fiber of your being?

Does it hold value or is it routine?

Do those words in themselves exploit true unconditional love?

Does he love you the way you want to be loved?

Or is he love itself.

Does he manifest every emotion within you?

Creating the safest place you have to hide, while exposing your biggest fear.

Has his world become you?

Does he give you all he ever had?

Does he give you....

What I couldn't?

Untitled:

There aren't enough daydreams in the day where I don't want to see your smiling face.

There isn't enough ticks on the clock where you don't invade my every thought.

Not enough words in the dictionary to give the world's greatest commentary....on your beauty.

Pictures don't do you justice...

I mean really it's just

That I admire all that you do

A queen of the throne handling hers and staying true.

To yourself and who you are

So are pictures really worth a thousand words.

Or is it I'm just trying to stay ahead of the curve.

And acknowledge you for what you're truly worth.

One of God's greatest creation to ever be put on earth.

<h1 style="text-align:center;">Truth?!:</h1>

What's funny is that two people are supposed to be in a relationship but yet they have to answer to everyone around them.

Not just his side but her side as well.

Her side "y aren't there pictures if you and him up" his side "what's the relationship with the father of her children". Aren't both deemed rude and exactly non of the other persons business.....

"You're always on your phone" and "You're always on Facebook" they scream at each other. Seems like there are a lot of double standards. "I hate how everyone tries to be in your business in this town". With that being said don't you think you should keep some things private?

It's funny how everyone has something to say but don't apply thier own advice to reflect in their lives. People don't want to be in the middle of shit but will kindly put their two cents in and look at you so they can get something back.

My Facebook page does not tell you who I am. Written words of the heart does. I don't make post to that page to tell you where I am or who I'm with simply because it is just that.

 A page.

People who have my number know what to say. I am divorced twice over. I am an alcoholic, I have a daughter, I've cheated, I've lost my faith, I've had cars repossessed, I've destroyed my credit. I've left a woman's side because I was afraid, I've gone to get counseling and help with dealing, being in the military. I've sat up all night watching helpessly as a seizures happen. I've not been the father I should be.

I've lacked in child support and in jobs. I've lied, been disrespected and have betrayed others. I know that there are people who look at my page and my girlfriends page to see if I am where I say I am.

 If I'm with this person or that person.

Run back to my family or even to her and say "he's hiding something".

The only thing I'm hiding is trying to protect my family. That means I don't tell everyone my business I talk to the people that matter and my circle is very small. I'm sorry that you didn't make the cut. But if you gladly scroll up you can read everything you want to know about me. And just for the ones who can't see it on my regular Facebook page I'll post it there too.

Now please do me a favor

Go run tell that!

Surroundings:

I wish everything could be black and white. Not talking about race or actual color. Just matters of life, or maybe just matters of heart.

How when you need someone so badly that your body is torn to shreds when you are apart.

Or maybe just allowing the other person to be able to understand you. Not just who you are. But the trauma and your surroundings that shaped you.

Maybe being misunderstood is a good thing. Because when those flashing lights on the camera go off no one can see the pain.

And yet how could they? Sitting in a room full of people as you clutch to your drink as the only tangible substance that's in you reach.

Keeping your mind from wondering and letting people see glimpses of who you really are. You wave say "hi" and move through the crowd as you make your way to the bar.

What is love? Is it a belief, faith, hope or just a feeling? How do you know? Is there a rule book? Is there a blueprint for building a path to this thing in my chest that's beating?

I look around at my surroundings and become physically and spiritually detached. I rise up above the crowd, my body, and the earth. Heart racing, body scared feeling I as if I'm about to collapse.

I start to panic, but then I hear your voice as you say "I'm here, I'll always be here". I look up and I see you floating in the distance with your arm stretch out and your hand extended.

You then say "it's here whenever you're ready". My mouth is dry I take a deep breath. I slowly begin to make my descent back towards earth, the crowd, and my shell. Not knowing if I'll ever be ready.

Torn between what's right and what I feel I want, actually feels like a need.
Like blood in my veins, another person's touch, or the air I need to breath.

Again though it's not just black and white. The same thing that is making us regret, feel nauseous, pain, heartache. Is the very same thing that gave us this precious gift of a new Life.

Sometimes:

Sometimes I can't put you into words. Sometimes you make me forget the words I want to say.

Sometimes my brain shuts off after you kiss me.

Sometimes I wonder why it is, you want to be with me.

Sometimes I'm thankful for you. Sometimes I don't think I deserve you. Sometimes I try to imagine my life without you.... sometimes..

The truth is that sometimes equals all the time.

So all the time I can't possibly imagine my life without you.

And all the time I thank God for you. But sometimes I just want to stay in the moment with you....

Yea Sometimes

Perfection:

She has the walk that makes the flame of a candle jealous.

Her touch is the very meaning of enchantment.

Her eyes are the vast oceans of pure truthful emotions.

Her voice cannot be measured by any note played by an instrument or nature.

Her hair is to be compared to only the finest silk.

Her skin bathed in butter milk then sweetened with a touch of honey.

Her lips bittersweet: orgasmic as in tasting a forbidden fruit. Painful to pull away from.

Her smell is hypnotic casting a spell on your mind until she's all you think about.

Things that I day dream about when I think about the perfect woman....

Things that I think about.....
When I think about you.

You Should Know:

So I have so many things I want to tell you but I can't
find the right order in which to do so.

I want to tell you about it all.

How I was sitting on top of the world, to when I lost myself, I stumbled, I fell

excuse me I'm sorry ,failed.

I want to tell you of my heroic tales of bravery and justice.

On the other hand are disappointment and betrayl

of people who have given me their trust.

I want to tell you my past is just like all the other boys you've dated.

But my present is a man with strength and love.

My future is that of a family that of trust, honor, and loyalty.

I want to share with you everything that has made me who I am

things that always encourage me to be better.

I want to be a better human, friend, brother, son, father, boyfriend,
husband, lover, man of God...

Just a better man.

I wish I could tell you the all of things I'm thinking about.

All of the ways I want you and all of the doors in my mind that lead to you.

My heart is so torn on my belief on if I deserve you or should I embrace you.

The fear in my mind doesn't out way the love in my
heart. All I'm really trying to say I guess is.

I love you and I'm in love with you.

That it is greater than the moon and back, but more on a level of
more than every star in the universe, every grain of sand in the
world and more than every molecule of water that exists.

I just thought you should know.

Social Prayer:

I hope the pages of Facebook keep you warm at night

May the hundreds of likes on photo shopped and perfect angled pictures help hide the truth of who you really are.

May all of your comments on what you had for breakfast, what your baby mama and/or baby daddy did or didn't do for you, and the stalkers that flood your inbox complete your day.

May your time stamps and check ins reflect exactly where you are at all times and also take moments away that are truly special since you have to upload the pictures you took right now.

May the pages of Instagram give you the hopes of one day in being so self preserved. That no one can see you or even come close to you.

May your post reflect a world that isn't filled with truth. Instead filled with misguided or misdirected points on how you say someone else is feeling a certain way. When truthfully you can't even express how you feel.

May the pages of your tablet, laptop, and phone provide you with all the interaction that you need. In order to keep real people at a distance along with human interaction.

These are the things we pray to social media sometimes.

Amen

Wonder

Do you ever sit and wonder

 I mean really wonder about life.

Wonder about what it would be like to find true happiness.

To wake up and be completely content with the life you're leading.

Wonder what it feels like to hold value

 someone looking forward to having you in their lives.

Wonder what life would be like if it was never cloudy

if it never stormed again.

Everyday, no matter what is filled with self appreciation

Making life worth living.

Do you ever wonder about true peace.

Never doubting the reason for your existence.

Spend time wondering about the goals you've set

 Wasting time trying to figure out if you're the person/human being you were supposed to be.

Wondering about your time spent

if it was ever impactful to someone other than yourself.

I too have sat and wondered about these things.

But a couple days ago I just realized

I don't have to.

Blessed to have my wondering mind at ease

when God sent me you.

Alone:

I'm here
No I'm not
I want to be
I can't
Don't love me
I can't be loved
I want to be loved
Need to be loved
I fall short every time
Faced with frozen emotions
Misunderstanding self
I'm alone

Inside of myself
Guilt, doubt and fear
Remain
Distrust of myself
Indecisive choices
Ideas still in the dark
Talking to myself
Relying on myself
For answers I cannot provide
Myself
I'm alone

Reality
Isn't real
Vision and dreams
Become my reality
Become me
Loss of control
Betrayed
By my eyes
My ears
My mind
In a war
That never ends
I fight on both sides
I'm alone
Is it time
To create
Display

CHAVEZ LAPORTÉ CAMPBELL

The ultimate
Treasonous act
Against one self
Self destruction
Illusion of freedom
Faint heart beat
I'm alone

Working:

So what's a man supposed to do.

Trying to be a father, a friend

A husband, a dependable

and reliable business man.

Heavy is the head that wears the crown.

Making sure my kids always have food to eat.

Always trying to provide so it never rains on their faces while they sleep.

But at last it seems to be the death of me.

Wagering in on a war within myself. The odds are stacked against me.

How can I be so successful in a place of business and yet not be able to discover who my children are as people.

I want to rule the world and have it in my grasp.

But yet I can't even hold on to what's in front of me.

A young man with a dream that seems impossible to reach.

I keep dropping the ball each time a pass is made to me.

Simply because I keep believing that my past has become the substance and existence of me.

I have failed in trying to be who I'm expected to be.

I have failed in trying to be who I want to be.

So I stand here alone, messed up, confused, and full of regrets.

Seeing my reflection not in the mirror but in people's eye's.

Labeled as the imperfection.

I walk with my head down and continue my path without any hesitation.

I continue to move forward

For me

For my family

For God

The fact is that all I'm good at.

All that I can truly say I am.

Is just a hard working man.

Strangers:

It's you I know it
It has to be......right?
The reason why I have all these sleepless nights!
I can't get you out of my mind
So the next time I see you
I'll be sure to say hi!

And I did
I'm so blessed to have you, waking up next to you everyday
I watch you as you sleep
Making sure you're ok
Then going down the hall and checking on the babies
Three boys and two girls making our circle of life
Complete as our hearts over flow with love
Because we have all the love to give

Each in every time I think about our love and our family
It brings me to tears
We dated for a couple of years
Before I was able to conquer my fears
Remembering the look in your fathers eyes
As I ask him for permission for you to be my wife

We use to spend countless hours on the phone
Falling more in love with you
Giving my heart to you
And finally being able to call you "Home"

Remember all the laughter and the love that we shared
Never met someone who is able to care
The way that you do
Never giving up on love or us
And having complete trust
in me too

Yea we struggled at first
Two very different personalities
But do to our affection
We were able to create new tendencies
There was no distance that could tear us apart
No words left unspoken
battle scars from how hard we fought
In order to stay completely unbroken

All because of one click on a computer
My life changed, my soul changed
And would stay this way forever

Thank you for the faith in me when I was down
Thank you for the strength you had in me
To pick me off the ground.
I love you so much I want to shout it to the world
Let everyone know that this is my one and only:
My girl..........

Sigh.......It's you right?
You're the reasons for all of my sleepless nights
I wish that all of this had happened
And that I was your man
But the truth of the matter is
You don't know who I am

I can't work up the nerves to say
"Hello Ma'am"
My heart races and my palms are filled with sweat
We are still strangers to each other
Simply because we haven't met.

Makes Sense:

I can see life with you
 does that make sense?
Not a life
 Life itself
the living aspect of it.
Where each and every day I need you apart of it.
 From the very beginning to the very end.
Your voice,
your touch,
 your opinion,
your guidance,
your love,
your care,
your friendship,
your faith,
your honesty,
your companionship.
These are needs not wants,
these are blessings,
Each day I have you, I'm more than a man,
more than a superhero,
more powerful than a king

Having you by my side has made me realize that no one has remotely come within an inkling to the way my heart beats for you.

It's filled with the most passionate love of all love.

I am petrified at the very thought of losing you for any reason.

I miss laying next to you whenever I'm not there.

I miss how you don't breath at first when we are done making love.

I miss the way you smile whenever I'm talking to the kids.

I love the way you get dimples in your cheeks, both sets.

I love that you are always willing and wanting to try new things.

I long for you everyday, every hour, every minute, every second.

There isn't a war that I wouldn't go through or too if it meant I was coming home to you.

Home, home, you are home to me.

You're my heart and I always want to be where my heart is.

I have never given myself completely to any, you make me feel as if there is no choice.

God gave me you

you require all of me

you expect and will accept nothing less from me.

It scares me to death

I'm so afraid of failing,

even more devastated by the idea of not trying

Every part of you is now a part of me.

I want to be better

with you

for you.

for Us

Makes sense?

Explain:

When you see him, what happens?

Does time fight against you?

Do you yearn to be closer?

Does the air become thick and opaque?

When he touches you what do you feel?

Does every hair on the back of your neck stand?

Do goosebumps flood your entire body like a broken levee?

When he kisses you, do your taste buds rejoice?

Does your heart stop with each kiss reviving yourself as he pulls away?

When he looks into your eyes, does love reflect in them?

Is it a glimpse of the future, or is it destiny?

Has it been written?

When he makes love to you, are you transcended?

Do you completely give him everything?

As your bodies completely inelastically collide....is that where you want to stay forever?

When he says "I love you" does it touch every fiber of your being?

Does it hold value or is it routine?

Do those words in themselves exploit true unconditional love?

When you read this, do you feel him?

Do you breathe him in?

Do you need him?

When you read this.....

Who do you see?

Is it me?

Searching:

I'm lost and I'm shaken, sipping from this glass of elixir I'm drinking
You said I'd never be forsaken
I can't find you in any picture...
That's been taken.

Reading directly from the scripture
I'm alone and with my heart punctured
Crying out
As I'm bleeding out
Filling my wounds with dirt.

I put out who I am on written word
Chasing the vision I see as perfect.
Causing chaos and mayhem...
I wonder...
Is it worth it
I open my mouth to speak
As my hands lift up to reach
But there's to much phlegm

I look up as if to see you
Eyes clouded by the storm
Not feeling reborn
Rather torn
Where's my strength that comes from you?

This flesh is only worn as a mask
To cover up what I can't grasp
Everything I can't confess.
Non the less....
You see!

But you're supposed too.
And in my time of need
I'm supposed to cling to you.
Thoughts of suicide
Have seemed to occupy
The life you gave.
I feel so strange
In this maze
Of emotion and conflict.
Were you able to predict
That I'd become an addict
And afflict
Destruction
On the love
That you've surrounded me with?

God fearing, the son of a preacher.
Looking for the father
In his place a teacher.
Not unappreciative
Of the life lessons;
Still listening and hesitant
Prayers will bring progression.

In the presence of many audiences
Tears fall continuously.
My faith in you is broken.
How could this be?
I'm your chosen.

Questioning you...
My one and only maker
I just need to be reset;
Blown fuse:
Circuit breaker

Busting out in cold sweats.
You said I'd have nothing to lose
No regrets.
Eternal life is what I stand to gain.
Yet neglected to tell me
All the strife and pain.

Awake; I Am

Peering straight into the darkness, like my eyes are wide shut. Unfamiliar sounds in the distance surrounding me.
Echos of screaming victims and vengeance riding laughter piercing depths of my soul. My legs move slow and as if each weighed a thousand pounds.

I drive my footsteps into the thick mushy terrain. My clothes soaked, my body on fire. I would offer sacrifice but all of my blood has been taken by ticks and leeches. I scream as loud as I can for help but in return, only given silence.

My scars, my sores burn and itch. As if I dived into to a lake filled with a mutated chickenpox virus then sprayed with salt water. I claw at my skin. Rendering pieces of flesh torn away from muscle and bone. I peel the layer of skin back like an orange exposing the truth hidden underneath.

Things not visible to the naked eye, things that have been repressed in the soul. I continue to claw, tear, peel and unwind each individual muscle. All that is left are bones. In the darkness a flame ignites, burning what use to be apart of me in this swamp.

Random Quotes

" Written Words of

ifyoucouldseemeknowimshortbuttallflipthatpatthatpattycakeapple-
jacksshoutouttothepaignbeeasyandnongreasysmellthatchickenhungergames-
thesunishotbirdmanbirdmanturnup

your heart"

Wait........what?

Finished:

Its finished right? Or is it I sit here and I wish I had a drink to numb me from all the pain that I feel inside each and everyday. I wake up and it's a constant reminder of what I've fucked up and what I have done wrong.

I'm always on edge I don't know how to live sober and the very thought of what tomorrow may bring is enough to make me want to just give up. Every decision I have mad has been a fucked up one. People told me that we were good together and that we would be for life.

The crazy thing is I can't even remember half of the time we spent together. I don't know how to cope with all the bills I haven't paid. I don't know how to begin to express love or accept it. I pick up a pen or a pencil and I want to write music. I can hear it loud and clear but then as soon as I touch my pencil to the page it stops.

I'm going insane

I have lost my mind.

I can only accept what people tell me to. Feeling like a baby that's about to take their first step. Apprehensive and nervous, no clue as to what the fuck is going on. I don't have any one to run to, or maybe it's the fact that I don't want to let them in. Maybe I'm destined to be alone walking like a time bomb that's ticking to blow up on the next heart I get.

The results are always the same. Give hurt, apologize, get hurt, accept apology. I'm dazed and confused on why my parents mean so much to you but when it comes to me you could give a shit or two. Did you call to let me know how happy you are, did you want to rub it in my face. You set me up to receive this hurt. You gave my father the loaded gun so all he had to do was pull the trigger.

I don't know who I am without the bottle I don't know if I'm even a good father. Haven't spoken to my daughter in months. I don't even know what her voice sounds like or what her favorite show is. I don't remember, if I had a drink I could bring it up but since I'm sober I don't know what to say. AND YOU KNOW THIS DON'T YOU.

This is why you got out when you had the chance no longer having to accept anyone that is less than a man. That can give you what you need and want from life. Not just enjoying his or destroying yours.

Forever calling you his wife. April 17, the day I became sober. I've never cried so many times before in my life. I don't even know why I'm here or what I'm doing here. I have lied and cheated to so many people no one will trust me.....they can't.

I'm so disgusted with myself I believe I should have to do everything on my own. Maybe it's what I need....or maybe I'll just end up being a drunk. I quit everything I've ever done. The military, being a husband, being a boyfriend, being a son, being a......father.

I now see what I truly am for the first time. We are supposed to be made in Gods image but how can that be if I'm like this? You, my father, and everyone else was right. I seem to be incapable of love. I think everyone sees and knows that now.

Open Chat:

To everyone that I love, I'm sorry for not telling you that I love you on a daily bases but this world sucks ass.......

"I feel the same way?"

Do you?

"Yes!"

"When I was younger I was raped by a person who I trusted with all of my heart. I don't want to go into details but he was my uncle."

"Hello"

Yes

"Since we are sharing loss, I want to tell you how it feels to lose both parents to cancer within months of each other"

I'm sorry to hear.....

"Hey"

Yes

"I was deployed in Iraq, I've shot and killed innocent women and children. Carry that around with you everyday."

That breaks my heart how do you cope with......

"I have a story for you"

Yes

"Try being an drug addict, literally pushing all of your family away just so I can get high in my car or behind any building. What's even more heartbreaking is that I have a daughter, but I can't even remember her name. I'll probably never be able to tell you the color of her eyes"

Wow I can't imagine having to deal with that......

"I see a lot of people sharing their stories on here, I would like to share"

Yea go ahead

"I and my kids have been homeless for over two years now. We come to the shelter and I am able to use the computer get them a hot meal and a warm place to sleep. Anyway it's just me because my husband lost his job and we lost everything. Shortly after that.....he killed himself"

OH MY GOD......I don't know what say.....

"I'll tell you what to say. How about watching your family die in a fire, because you were too afraid to go in and try to save them. After they put the flames out. I had to go identify each and everyone of my family members. My mom, my dad, and my brother and sister"

....

"This guy seems speechless, try having all of your children get killed in a church van accident on their way to summer bible school. I buried all three of my kids. Do you know what helps ease the pain alcohol"

No that's not the answer. I was starting this chat room just to vent and show my frustration with not having money or a job but I now see that's the least of my problems. Is everyone ok?

"No we're not ok"

"I'm done with this world it's time for me to end it"

"I can't live without my children"

"I see fire everywhere I turn I can't take it anymore"

"Fireworks sound like gunshots I see their faces everywhere I turn"

"I just need one more fix"

"God took my parents just to watch me suffer"

Wait everyone hold on
Just talk to me I'm willing to listen we can figure all of this out. Just stay in the chat room with me

Hello???

Hello??????

Anyone please say something...........

Respire:

Days past nights past
Time stands still

New friends turn into old friends
Old friends turn into distance
Distance manifests oceans

Tears yielding from pain
Pain acquiring attention
Attention taking breaths away
Slowly

Calmness breeds terror
Terror amplifies panic
Panic can create heroes

Please enjoy a preview of the upcoming series. "The Letter"

"The Letter"
Part 1 of the series coming in June 2021

The Letter: Opening

Good Morning baby, well its afternoon here. I wanted to write this letter just to let you know that I am ok. I am surviving simply because the thought of you keeps me fighting. I woke up to the bitter dry air over here. Its so hot here but you get use to it after a while. You learn a few tricks to make yourself comfortable and still be efficient at getting the job done. Its cooler at night sometimes, but other nights it feels as if the sun didn't go down at all. It seems like no matter how many showers I take I don't feel quite clean enough. We had a sand storm a couple of days ago and I am still getting sand out of places I don't think it should be. I bet you just laughed at that last line. Anyway I sometimes find it hard to breath out here. It could be that I'm dehydrated or maybe its the fact that I have been gone already for 97 days. Not that I'm counting them. I find myself trying to count the hours instead. That way I can figure out if you're awake or at work or visiting your mom. It helps me over here sometimes.

I miss everything about you. Your laugh, the way your nose squishes up when you're mad at me. How you try to ignore me but then I just do something stupid to make you laugh. I miss your cooking. The galley here or the chow hall or mess decks, how ever you want to say it. Isn't all that great but it keeps us going. I'm still eating on those skittles you sent me in my care package. Gotta love skittles right? Before you even ask the answer is YES that is all I ate today but lunch is coming around soon and I will go eat then. I know your nose just squished up. I am taking care of myself so don't get mad. We don't have a good connection here for internet so I won't be able to skype just yet but when its up we will set up a skype date. Unfortunatlly I can't tell you where I am but its not where I was. Please don't ask me if its more dangerous then where I use to be. Things right now are calm, no rpg's, no hostile fire. We are still on high alert always ready to go at a moments notice. There is no such thing as total relaxation over here. To tell you the truth I'm still kind of jumpy. I am in a different mindset over here...hell we all are. You have to keep your emotions in check in order to make sure you live another day.

It's kind of weird because at the same time you never forget about your fallen brothers and sisters either. I know I am in the Navy but over here there isn't a separation of Navy, Marines, Air Force, or Army. We are all in this together and I have met so many different people from different walks of life and branches. We are a family over here I will die to protect them and I know they would do the same for me. In some ways I am closer to the people out here than my own family. I guess its because of the life or death situation over here. Just know that my plan is to come home to you alive. You're the reason why I'm fighting! Well and for US and everyone who has lost someone on 9/11. We will make them pay and we will never forget that day. I'm sorry I get so emotional about that day but you know it why I joined. I'm sorry for rambaling on and on so I guess I will just end this letter and get some chow. I love you very much and I have your picture with me always. I can't wait until I get to touch your face once again. Be safe baby as will I.

Your Love
Always and Forever

The Letter: Waiting

Good morning my love. I feel as if you have been gone for years even tho its only been 131 days but who's counting. The baby and I are doing well, I will say I was quite worried about you. The longer we go with out talking the more I stress out. I know it isn't good for the baby but damn I need you to come back to me alive. Since we are on the subject you know I've obviously have made it into the second trimester, on the way to the third,....I just wanted to let you know that you are having a babygirl!!!!! I hope you are as excited as I am. Which you are lol. We should start picking out names(great mind's think a like).

I want it to mean something so please don't allow your mom to make suggestions. Don't worry I'll keep my mom at bay as well lol. I'm so happy for you that you and Tyrrell are in the same unit?!, squadron?!, platoon?!....lol I forget what you call it. How's he doing? Does he like it? I bet he wants to come home with the quickness. Never seen him as a....a military man. I'm so bad with what you guys are called but I'm learning baby. Has Tyrrell seen any action yet? Please take care of him I know he's your friend but most of the time he's an idiot lol. You two need to be safe over there and I'll be sure to cook you up something special when you get back. And before your smartass says anything, yes I'm learning how to cook. Your mom has been teaching me so you can SUCK IT! I almost forgot to say thank you for the compliments you gave me in your letter. It's like I keep telling you baby, I'm only awesome and amazing because you are awesome and amazing.

Baby you complete me we are a walking example that God is real and that he continues to bless us each and every day. We are partners and no matter what I'll always be here for you. And you know I'm not just saying that. Don't take this the wrong way but I'm your real life bottom bitch. I have been here and I will continue to be here. When you wanted to drop out of high school I was there. Encouraging you to stay and finish. When you wanted to join the military, I wrote you every day in boot camp. Through the still birth of our child, the lonely sleepless nights, the anxiety if waiting by the phone just to hear your voice. It's me and it's always been me. God put us together and it will be God who has to take us apart. I love you with everything I am. As long as I get to be in your life and be your partner, lover, mother of your child, your number one, your all, your wife.....I'll be here waiting for you.

Just so you know! It makes my heart happy to hear you talk about finding God. I think that will definitely help us keep our love and faith very strong. So you want a care package or a "care package" lol. Well I'm feeling like a whale so I'm not sure if you'll be getting naked pics of me. I'm sure I can get to the skittles, snickers, and twizzlers that you need. Maybe I'll send you some of mom's cookies....then maybe send you a pic of mine(evil grin) lol. I should stop I just got done talking about God and we aren't even married yet. That's how we got in this predicament lol. Anyway you need to try to get some sleep hun, I know it's probably not that easy and I have no clue what's going on over there but can you just promise me you'll try? Even if it's false hope it makes me feel a little better...I'm begging you. Ok darling I really love you but this little girl is just dancing on my bladder. I love you more than you will ever know. I'm excited that you are excited about the baby. I'm really excited more for her though. Because she gets to see first hand how a man should treat and love a woman. You're wonderful, be blessed and be safe.

Love you always
Your one and only
Bottom Bitch.

www.ingramcontent.com/pod-product-compliance
Lightning Source LLC
Chambersburg PA
CBHW050956050726
47592CB00007B/2595